A Journey With Grief

A Son's Poignant and Personal Journey

By: David Laubert, DVM

Copyrights ©2025 by David Laubert, DVM

All Rights Reserved.

Dedication

Acknowledgements

This book began with a single idea—thank you to my friend, David, for planting it in my head. Thank you to my dear friend, Sue, who suggested the final tweak to the title. To Jim, thank you for holding space for both silence and sorrow. Your support is the quiet silence between the lines. To my parents, whose love and guidance have shaped me more than any syllable I've ever written and have been the scaffolding of my life, and the rhythm beneath these verses. To the readers of this book, I offer these fragments of grief to everyone who is carrying loss and searching for a language to hold it.

The cardinal's song

Reminds me of my mother

I miss her so much

Death makes a new norm

But now nothing seems normal

It makes me ponder

When a parent dies

It leaves such a void in us

It is so heavy

Death's impact is odd

Odd, I am a new me now

What will that look like?

Walks before sunrise

A free concert of bird songs

Time for reflection

Perpetual ache

The pain seems unreal sometimes

The cost of deep love

Parents are the glue

Now that they are both not here

Who will be the glue?

The first holiday

Where I can't call you to talk

It is still so raw

I am missing you

I feel you in wind, nature

You are everywhere

First, it was you, Mom

Now my precious Maggie Mae

Can I get through this?

Yesterday was hard

The heaviness lingering

Grief is physical

Chattering of birds

Excited for the new day

It is uplifting

Morning has arrived

When will grief hit me today

One can never know

Seems the end just waits

Waits quietly to be seen

Then the appearance

I long to see you

I look now in the moments

I know you are here

Grief is an odd thing

Desire to move past or through

But feel not able

You are gone from earth

The void is omnipresent

Memories so raw

Ugh, this hits so hard

Anticipatory grief

How to survive this

My chest is heavy

So much sadness to process

I am not okay

I miss you so much

In the noise, in the silence

It will not turn off

Grief, it's the process

It is not an emotion

It's relearning life

You can't outrun grief

It feels so raw and painful

Sit with it, feel it

We are different

On the other side of loss

A permanent change

Grief is derailed love

It's where to put that love now

It is so draining

I am feeling stuck

Between what was and what is

An internal fight

Literally changed

The losses are so profound

It's physical pain

I find grief to be

Like an intrusive sorrow

With no boundaries

Reframing my grief

You were here, and it mattered

My grief honors you

Sitting with my thoughts

Unpredictable feelings

But necessary

You left so quickly

I wasn't ready for it

I won't ever be

I want more with you

More walks, talks, laughs, moments, smiles

That I will not get

Grief, through pain and tears

Reminds us that love won't end

Ubiquitous love

It would not hurt so

If there weren't love for you still

And your love for me

A million moments

Of laughter, fun, love and smiles

They keep me going

Your death has changed me

Unimaginable ways

Unexpected ways

Grief does not vanish

It's part of who I am now

I'm forever changed

Your wings were ready

I was not, and still can't be

Juxtaposition

How can the absence

Be such a physical weight

Grief is so complex

I still can't fathom

You are actually gone

Acceptance is hard

Death redefines life

Now a before and after

A brutal divide

Grief is ambushing

Always such little notice

I never know when

Physically gone

Loss isn't just the absence

It is the silence

How does the absence

Feel empty and heavy now

The dichotomy

The thing about dogs

Is they accept our true selves

No pretense needed

The absence of you

Has now changed me forever

Permanent changes

Grief, for me, has been

Feeling like my world crumbled

And I can't fix it

Grief is a purchase

We never really wanted

Non-refundable

Grief is creative

Every day, it finds new ways

To sneak up on me

There are days when life

Just really feels like too much

The mind can be loud

You must let it hurt

You must let it not make sense

As long as it takes

We can't avoid grief

We must learn to carry it

Love was and is here

Try to ignore it

But grief will just wait for you

So don't ignore it

Grief, it makes me feel

Like, I don't recognize myself

Evolving daily

It's not easier

Grief is different each day

It's true for me, too

In the silent times

My heart aches with emptiness

Why is loss so loud?

Grief is more than pain

It's that nothing will ever

Be the same again

Simple tasks are hard

A detached, meaningless fog

Getting through routines

I think that grieving

Is like the last act of love

We show those we've lost

Grief makes you pretend

That you still somehow are strong

Yet you feel fragile

Healing can happen

The grief, you have to feel it

Whenever it comes

When we lost you, Mom

We lost ourselves that same day

Changed forevermore

I walk, talk, laugh, smile

Behind the smile and pretense

My heart is broken

Oh, sweet Maggie Mae

I miss you so much, too much

I could not heal you

Is it possible

To feel inner homelessness

Grief is so complex

I may always mourn

The missed opportunities

To spend time with you

Grief seems to be like

Learning to carry love and

Loss at the same time

Grief can be tricky

Exhaustion by sadness, but

Fearing its absence

Some days I function

Some days not so much, really

But both are okay

Death and grief are rude

Rarely a notice or sign

Arrive when they do

Often it's sadness

But also the heaviness

Grief's strange agenda

It is a strange thing

To feel everything yet

Also feel nothing

A journey of sorts

To discover a new path

Grief's evolution

Yes, the loss is hard

But I wouldn't trade the love

To avoid the grief

Grief has been a gap

Between who I was before

And who I am now

Some days are not bad

Others are not good at all

Grief waves are random

The ideation

Sometimes can be a bit much

Sharing is the key

It lives differently

In each of us who lives it

Grief is so unique

So odd to feel guilt

After a laugh or a smile

Does that ever change?

Grief has no U-turn

No going back to what was

Embrace the new you

Grief is exhausting

The pressure to seem okay

But want to not be

Grief, it makes you morph

You learn to dance in the storms

But storms don't pass

It is so tiresome

To act like I'm doing well

So others feel good

It is hard at times

To keep in mind that the grief

Is from love still felt

Time doesn't heal grief

Instead, it makes you wear it

So differently

At the funeral

You also say goodbye

To whom you once were

Some days I smile, move

It's the weight of pretending

That I am okay

www.ingramcontent.com/pod-product-compliance
Lightning Source LLC
Chambersburg PA
CBHW071143060526
44107CB00131B/187